TENDER MERCIES

As we are spiritually awake and alert we see
His hand in our lives -Neil L Andersen

TENDER MERCIES

TENDER MERCIES

TENDER MERCIES

TENDER MERCIES

The Lord bless you and keep you ~Numbers 6:24

TENDER MERCIES

TENDER MERCIES

TENDER MERCIES

TENDER MERCIES

TENDER MERCIES

TENDER MERCIES

TENDER MERCIES

TENDER MERCIES

Simple, consistent, good habits lead to a life
full of bountiful blessings -Richard G Scott

TENDER MERCIES

TENDER MERCIES

TENDER MERCIES

TENDER MERCIES

TENDER MERCIES

TENDER MERCIES

TENDER MERCIES

TENDER MERCIES

TENDER MERCIES

TENDER MERCIES

TENDER MERCIES

TENDER MERCIES

TENDER MERCIES

TENDER MERCIES

TENDER MERCIES

TENDER MERCIES

O Lord; may your loving kindness and your truth
always guard me ~Psalms 40:11

TENDER MERCIES

TENDER MERCIES

TENDER MERCIES

TENDER MERCIES

TENDER MERCIES

TENDER MERCIES

TENDER MERCIES

TENDER MERCIES

May He grant you your heart's desire and fulfill
all your plans ~Psalms 20:4

TENDER MERCIES

TENDER MERCIES

TENDER MERCIES

TENDER MERCIES

TENDER MERCIES

TENDER MERCIES

TENDER MERCIES

TENDER MERCIES

Great are your compassions, O Lord; revive me
according to your judgments -Psalms 119:156

TENDER MERCIES

TENDER MERCIES

TENDER MERCIES

TENDER MERCIES

TENDER MERCIES

TENDER MERCIES

TENDER MERCIES

TENDER MERCIES

Come, Thou fount of every blessing. Tune my heart
to sing thy grace -Robert Robinson

TENDER MERCIES

TENDER MERCIES

TENDER MERCIES

TENDER MERCIES

TENDER MERCIES

TENDER MERCIES

TENDER MERCIES

TENDER MERCIES

The tender mercies of the Lord are real and they
do not occur randomly or merely by coincidence
                                    -David A Bednar

TENDER MERCIES

TENDER MERCIES

TENDER MERCIES

TENDER MERCIES

TENDER MERCIES

TENDER MERCIES

TENDER MERCIES

TENDER MERCIES

TENDER MERCIES

TENDER MERCIES

TENDER MERCIES

Daily Reflections

DATE: NOTES:

Love beareth all things, believeth all things,
hopeth all things, endureth all things
~1 Corinthians 13:7

Daily Reflections

DATE: NOTES:

Daily Reflections

DATE: NOTES:

Daily Reflections

DATE: **NOTES:**

Daily Reflections

DATE: **NOTES:**

Daily Reflections

DATE: | NOTES:

Daily Reflections

DATE: NOTES:

Daily Reflections

DATE:	NOTES:

Daily Reflections

DATE: NOTES:

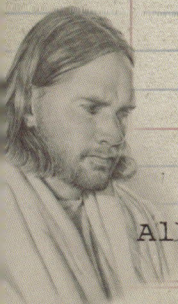

All things are possible to him who believes

~Mark 9:23

Daily Reflections

DATE:	NOTES:

Daily Reflections

DATE: NOTES:

Daily Reflections

DATE:	NOTES:

Daily Reflections

DATE: NOTES:

Daily Reflections

DATE:	NOTES:

Daily Reflections

DATE: **NOTES:**

Daily Reflections

DATE: NOTES:

Daily Reflections

DATE:	NOTES:

I have set the Lord continually before me

~Psalm 16:8

Daily Reflections

DATE:	NOTES:

Daily Reflections

DATE: NOTES:

Daily Reflections

DATE:	NOTES:

Daily Reflections

DATE: NOTES:

Daily Reflections

DATE:	NOTES:

Daily Reflections

DATE: **NOTES:**

Daily Reflections

DATE: NOTES:

Daily Reflections

DATE: NOTES:

Be still and know that I am God
~Psalms 46:10

Daily Reflections

DATE:	NOTES:

Daily Reflections

DATE: NOTES:

Daily Reflections

DATE:	NOTES:

Daily Reflections

DATE: NOTES:

Daily Reflections

DATE:	NOTES:

Daily Reflections

DATE: **NOTES:**

Daily Reflections

DATE:	NOTES:

Daily Reflections

DATE:	NOTES:

Do not let your heart be troubled;
believe in God, believe also in Me

~John 14:1

Daily Reflections

DATE:	NOTES:

Daily Reflections

DATE: NOTES:

Daily Reflections

DATE: | NOTES:

Daily Reflections

DATE: **NOTES:**

Daily Reflections

DATE: NOTES:

Daily Reflections

DATE: NOTES:

Daily Reflections

DATE:	NOTES:

Daily Reflections

DATE: NOTES:

Do not disbelieve, but believe

~John 20:27

Daily Reflections

DATE:	NOTES:

Daily Reflections

DATE: **NOTES:**

Daily Reflections

DATE:	NOTES:

Daily Reflections

DATE: NOTES:

Daily Reflections

DATE:	NOTES:

Daily Reflections

DATE: | NOTES:

Daily Reflections

DATE: | NOTES:

Daily Reflections

DATE: NOTES:

Choose for yourselves today whom you will serve

~Joshua 24:15

Daily Reflections

DATE:	NOTES:

Daily Reflections

DATE: | NOTES:

Daily Reflections

DATE:	NOTES:

Daily Reflections

DATE: NOTES:

Daily Reflections

DATE:	NOTES:

Daily Reflections

DATE: NOTES:

Daily Reflections

DATE: | NOTES:

Daily Reflections

DATE: **NOTES:**

Cast your burden upon the Lord

~Psalms 55:22

Daily Reflections

DATE:	NOTES:

Daily Reflections

DATE: NOTES:

Daily Reflections

DATE:	NOTES:

Daily Reflections

DATE: NOTES:

Daily Reflections

DATE: | NOTES:

Daily Reflections

DATE: NOTES:

Daily Reflections

DATE:	NOTES:

Daily Reflections

DATE: NOTES:

Take courage; I have overcome the world

~John 16:33

Daily Reflections

DATE:	NOTES:

Daily Reflections

DATE:　　NOTES:

Daily Reflections

DATE:	NOTES:

Daily Reflections

DATE: NOTES:

Daily Reflections

DATE:	NOTES:

Daily Reflections

DATE: NOTES:

Daily Reflections

DATE:	NOTES:

Daily Reflections

DATE: NOTES:

For we walk by faith, not by sight

~2 Corinthians 5:7

Daily Reflections

DATE:	NOTES:

Daily Reflections

DATE: | NOTES:

Daily Reflections

DATE:	NOTES:

Daily Reflections

DATE: NOTES:

Daily Reflections

DATE: NOTES:

Daily Reflections

DATE: | NOTES:

Daily Reflections

DATE: **NOTES:**

Daily Reflections

DATE: NOTES:

Delight yourself in the Lord;
And He will give you the desires of your heart
~Psalms 37:4

Daily Reflections

DATE:	NOTES:

Daily Reflections

DATE: NOTES:

Daily Reflections

DATE:	NOTES:

Daily Reflections

DATE: NOTES:

Daily Reflections

DATE:	NOTES:

Daily Reflections

DATE: NOTES:

Daily Reflections

DATE:	NOTES:

Daily Reflections

DATE: NOTES:

Daily Reflections

DATE:	NOTES:

Daily Reflections

DATE: NOTES:

Love is patient and kind
~1 Corinthians 13:4

Daily Reflections

DATE:	NOTES:

Daily Reflections

DATE: NOTES:

Daily Reflections

DATE:	NOTES:

Daily Reflections

DATE: | NOTES:

Daily Reflections

DATE:	NOTES:

Daily Reflections

DATE: NOTES:

Daily Reflections

DATE:	NOTES:

Daily Reflections

DATE: NOTES:

Daily Reflections

DATE:	NOTES:

Daily Reflections

DATE: **NOTES:**

Faith, hope, and love abide, these three;
but the greatest of these is love
~1 Corinthians 13:13

Daily Reflections

DATE:	NOTES:

Daily Reflections

DATE: NOTES:

Daily Reflections

DATE:	NOTES:

Daily Reflections

DATE: NOTES:

Daily Reflections

DATE: NOTES:

Daily Reflections

DATE: NOTES:

Daily Reflections

DATE: NOTES:

Daily Reflections

DATE: NOTES:

Daily Reflections

DATE:	NOTES:

Daily Reflections

DATE: **NOTES:**

For by grace you have been saved through faith

~Ephesians 2:8

Daily Reflections

DATE:	NOTES:

Daily Reflections

DATE: | NOTES:

DATE: | NOTES:

Daily Reflections

DATE:	NOTES:

Daily Reflections

DATE: NOTES:

Daily Reflections

DATE:	NOTES:

Daily Reflections

DATE: NOTES:

Daily Reflections

DATE:	NOTES:

Daily Reflections

DATE: NOTES:

Daily Reflections

DATE:	NOTES:

Daily Reflections

DATE: NOTES:

We love Him, because He first loved us
~1 John 4:19

Daily Reflections

DATE: NOTES:

Daily Reflections

DATE:	NOTES:

Daily Reflections

DATE:	NOTES:

Daily Reflections

DATE: NOTES:

Daily Reflections

DATE:	NOTES:

Daily Reflections

DATE: NOTES:

Daily Reflections

DATE:	NOTES:

Daily Reflections

DATE: **NOTES:**

Daily Reflections

DATE:	NOTES:

Daily Reflections

DATE: NOTES:

You will know the truth,
and the truth will make you free

~John 8:32

Daily Reflections

DATE:	NOTES:

Daily Reflections

DATE: | NOTES:

Daily Reflections

DATE:	NOTES:

Daily Reflections

DATE: NOTES:

Daily Reflections

DATE:	NOTES:

Daily Reflections

DATE: NOTES:

Daily Reflections

DATE:	NOTES:

Daily Reflections

DATE: NOTES:

Daily Reflections

DATE:	NOTES:

Daily Reflections

DATE: NOTES:

The Lord is my shepherd: I shall not want

~Psalms 23

Daily Reflections

DATE:	NOTES:

Daily Reflections

DATE:	NOTES:

Daily Reflections

DATE:	NOTES:

Daily Reflections

DATE: NOTES:

Daily Reflections

DATE: NOTES:

Daily Reflections

DATE: NOTES:

Daily Reflections

DATE:	NOTES:

Daily Reflections

DATE: NOTES:

Daily Reflections

DATE:	NOTES:

Daily Reflections

DATE:	NOTES:

Watch over your heart with all diligence

~Proverbs 4:23

Daily Reflections

DATE: NOTES:

Daily Reflections

DATE: NOTES:

Daily Reflections

DATE: NOTES:

Daily Reflections

DATE: NOTES:

Daily Reflections

DATE:	NOTES:

Daily Reflections

DATE: | NOTES:

Daily Reflections

DATE:	NOTES:

Daily Reflections

DATE: **NOTES:**

Daily Reflections

DATE:	NOTES:

Daily Reflections

DATE:	NOTES:

Those who wait for the Lord will gain
new strength   ~Isaiah 40

Daily Reflections

DATE:	NOTES:

Daily Reflections

DATE: **NOTES:**

Daily Reflections

DATE:	NOTES:

Daily Reflections

DATE: NOTES:

Daily Reflections

DATE:	NOTES:

Daily Reflections

DATE: **NOTES:**

Daily Reflections

DATE:	NOTES:

Daily Reflections

DATE:	NOTES:

For by grace you have been saved through faith

~Ephesians 2:8

Daily Reflections

DATE:	NOTES:

Daily Reflections

DATE: | NOTES:

Daily Reflections

DATE:	NOTES:

Daily Reflections

DATE: NOTES:

Daily Reflections

DATE:	NOTES:

Daily Reflections

DATE: **NOTES:**

Daily Reflections

DATE:	NOTES:

Daily Reflections

DATE: NOTES:

Daily Reflections

DATE:	NOTES:

Daily Reflections

DATE: **NOTES:**

If God is for us, who can be against us

~Romans 8:31

Daily Reflections

DATE:	NOTES:

Daily Reflections

DATE:	NOTES:

Daily Reflections

DATE:	NOTES:

Daily Reflections

DATE: NOTES:

Daily Reflections

DATE: | NOTES:

Daily Reflections

DATE: NOTES:

Daily Reflections

DATE:	NOTES:

Daily Reflections

DATE:	NOTES:

God will supply all your needs
~Phillipians 4:19

Daily Reflections

DATE:	NOTES:

Daily Reflections

DATE: NOTES:

Daily Reflections

DATE:	NOTES:

Daily Reflections

DATE: NOTES:

Daily Reflections

DATE:	NOTES:

Daily Reflections

DATE: **NOTES:**

Daily Reflections

DATE:	NOTES:

Daily Reflections

DATE: **NOTES:**

For God so loved the world
~John 3:16

Daily Reflections

DATE:	NOTES:

Daily Reflections

DATE: NOTES:

Daily Reflections

DATE: **NOTES:**

Daily Reflections

DATE: NOTES:

Daily Reflections

DATE:	NOTES:

Daily Reflections

DATE: NOTES:

Daily Reflections

DATE: **NOTES:**

Daily Reflections

DATE:	NOTES:

Peace I leave with you; My peace I give to you;
not as the world gives do I give to you
~John 14:27

Daily Reflections

DATE:	NOTES:

Daily Reflections

DATE: NOTES:

Daily Reflections

DATE: | NOTES:

Daily Reflections

DATE: | NOTES:

Daily Reflections

DATE: **NOTES:**

Daily Reflections

DATE: **NOTES:**

Daily Reflections

DATE:	NOTES:

Daily Reflections

DATE:	NOTES:

God is my strong fortress

~2 Samuel 22:33

Daily Reflections

DATE: NOTES:

Daily Reflections

DATE: NOTES:

Daily Reflections

DATE:	NOTES:

Daily Reflections

DATE: | NOTES:

Daily Reflections

DATE:	NOTES:

Daily Reflections

DATE: **NOTES:**

Daily Reflections

DATE:	NOTES:

Daily Reflections

DATE: **NOTES:**

Greater love has no one than this

~John 15:13

Daily Reflections

DATE: | NOTES:

Daily Reflections

DATE: NOTES:

Daily Reflections

DATE:	NOTES:

Daily Reflections

DATE:	NOTES:

Daily Reflections

DATE:	NOTES:

Daily Reflections

DATE:	NOTES:

Daily Reflections

DATE: **NOTES:**

Daily Reflections

DATE:	NOTES:

Treat others the way you want them to treat you

~Luke 6:31

Daily Reflections

DATE:	NOTES:

Daily Reflections

DATE:　NOTES:

Daily Reflections

DATE: **NOTES:**

Daily Reflections

DATE: **NOTES:**

Daily Reflections

DATE:	NOTES:

Daily Reflections

DATE: NOTES:

Daily Reflections

DATE:	NOTES:

Daily Reflections

DATE: NOTES:

All things you ask in prayer, believing,
you will receive   ~Matthew 21:22

Daily Reflections

DATE:	NOTES:

Daily Reflections

DATE: NOTES:

Daily Reflections

DATE:	NOTES:

Daily Reflections

DATE:	NOTES:

Daily Reflections

DATE:	NOTES:

Daily Reflections

DATE: | NOTES:

Daily Reflections

DATE: **NOTES:**

KINDNESS

COMPASSION

MERCY

love

TRUST

Grace

HAPPY

PEACE

Hope

 JOY